Unpoetic Lines

Volume II

Kate Chukwuemeka

BookLeaf Publishing

India | USA | UK

Dedication

For my wonderful husband, Pascal, and my beautiful daughter, Zaniya. You make my heart complete.

Preface

Acknowledgements

1. My Everyday

It's you, there's nothing else to say
Except, it's you.
that I want next to me
In all I do.
It's you, I want to be old with
Reminiscing on our favourite day
But Just not yet
I won't wish our time away
Because it's you, I want to laugh with
I wish I could pause every smile
So that time might slow down
And we can enjoy this for a while
Because it's you
There's nothing else to say
Except, it's you
That I want to be my everyday

2. Love Isn't a Choice

I don't think love is a choice
I don't know how it could be
When one day, suddenly
You were everything to me
I didn't choose to jump
I've always been too scared
Of where I may land
what if I am unprepared?
So, no, I don't think love is a choice
I think it is an accidental trip
A tumble, an icy skid
Off of a chalky cliff
Hoping that the waves below
Will be rocky enough to catch you
But calm enough that you won't drown
Hope is all you can do
Hope that the perfect balance
Of the unpredictable sea
Leaves you unscarred
And allows you to be free
To swim to shore, knowing
We don't choose love, it's a free fall
It just arrives, unannounced
Suddenly, you're my everything, my all

3. I Want

I want to lay in bed
Tracing words on your skin
As you drift off to sleep
My heart is already *all in*
I want your hand
Interwoven in mine
As we drive home
Counting every road sign
I want it to be you
That kisses my forehead
That looks at me just to smile
That means every word you've said
I want midnight kisses
Under bright firework skies
Enwrapped in a blanket of stars
I'm yours, from sunset to sunrise

4. Stained Pages

I have a thousand notebooks
Each of the pages stained
With details of every heartbreak
With my every bad decision, shamed
And there have been many
I wish I could replace
A million half rhymes
I wish I could just erase
I have a thousand notebooks
Detailing every storm as they rage
Just useless words, until I met you
The perfect rhyme on a stain-filled page

5. Your Poem

I could write you a poem
I could even make it rhyme
I could spend hours
Cultivating the perfect line
Just so you could know
Exactly what you mean to me
Exactly how my heart feels
Exactly what I see
Because when I look at you
I see safety, I see home
When I look at you
I know I will never be alone
But my words will never be enough
To explain exactly how I feel
Or how perfect you are
All I know is, you make love real

6. Always

When I say that I will always love you
I mean it, from the bottom of my heart
Always, I will love you
Longer than until death do we part
But what is always?
Always is the moments that hurt the most
And the height of happiness
Always is days, we both just coast
On waves with no real threat
But no real adrenaline peak
Always is the everyday
The ever-growing peace, we seek
Now what is love?
Love is the prayers we say every night
The way you smile at me
The way you hold me tight
Love is the laughter we share
And the kindness in your heart
Love is every second I spend with you
The peace you've given me from the start
So, where is peace?
Peace is found in your eyes and in your arms
Peace is found in your heart
And our interlocked palms

So, when I say I will love you always
It is less simple than it seems
It's a love that's deeper than oceans
And brighter than sunbeams
Always, a simple word
Always, I will love you
So, In this life and the next
I will say, I do

7. Always II

When I say I love you always
I don't think you realise what I mean
Because words are not enough
To shed light on a heart's unseen
When I say always, I mean
Until the last star is burnt out dust
And there is a fire raging
Destroying the earths crust
I will love you in the rain
And while the sun scorches my heart
Because a love so strong lives longer
than until when death forces us to part
When I say always, I mean
My heart would sooner give out
Than give up on my love for you
There is no doubt
I will love you on the next earth
When this one is no more
Through any storm your smile
Will always remain the one I adore
Words are far too simple
To truly grasp a hearts devotion
Like man cannot fathom
The depths of the ocean

I cannot begin to tell you
The breadth or the height
Or the weight of my love
You're the one I pray for every night
I will love you as long as my spirit lives
Even after my last breath
Because love is the only thing
Able to escape death
So I hope you always know
Every day that's starts anew
I thank God for giving me
Someone to love like you

8. Thankful Heart

With a heart full of love
I thank God for you everyday
You've made my life complete
There's not much else to say
Except you've made whole a heart
I thought no one could
If I could choose to fall in love with you
Over and over, I would
Just to give you half of what you deserve
I would steal the stars from the sky
Dive to the deepest part of the ocean
Anything to not live in your goodbye
I thank God for you
Every single day
With useless words that never mean
Exactly what I wish I could say

9. Unshakable

Time can force mountains to dust
Break down the toughest stone
But my love for you
Will be your forever home
Fires can scorch the earth
And oceans engulf the land
But there will never be a day
Where I won't hold your hand
I will love you until the world is no more
My love for you is unbreakable
It can weather any storm
My love for you, unshakable
The earth may cease to exist
But my love more fierce than a burning sun
Is infinite, boundless in nature
It cannot be undone

10. Gold Rings & Permanent Markers

Marriage is not the gold
That sits upon my hand
It's the interweaving of hearts
That long to understand
What the other feels
It's the laughter we share
In the midst of frustration
The consistence care
The vows we spoke are more than words
A promise of until death do we part
An etching of your name
In permanent marker on my heart

11. Dear Baby

Dear baby,
One day you'll be here
And we'll be complete
As we hold you near
I hope you know
How much daddy loves you
He has the kindness soul
For us, there's nothing he wouldn't do
Your daddy is the greatest man
I have ever met, my greatest love
And just like you
He is my blessing from above
And with every thought of you both
I thank God, for what he has done
The light you've both brought into my life
Is brighter than the burning sun
I will praise God every day
For giving me you like he gave me your dad
He saw the space in my heart
He gave me a family to make my heart glad

12. Dear Baby II

Dear baby,
We cannot wait to meet you
To see if your eyes
Are brown or green or blue
To watch as you grow
Your first smile, your first yawn
To sing you to sleep
Watch over you from dusk til dawn
Love is an understatement
Words could never suffice
For the way ours heart feels
We would protect you with our life
So baby, stay safe
Because you can be sure
This is love before first sight
Every inch of you, we already adore

13. Whisper From the Womb

I wonder what it's like for you
For me it's a whisper from the womb
Thoughts of who you might be
A flower waiting to bloom
Do you feel the same?
Do you hear my gentle laughter?
Do you dance to my heartbeat?
Do you long for our happily ever after?
Because I have dreamed of you forever
Your heart, your eyes, your face
Every inch of you is already perfect
There's not an ounce, I could replace
While I wait for the day
I finally get to hold you
I leave you with my heartbeat
It's all I can do
A melody with it own rhythm
Your personal lullaby
To let you now, I will always be here
To wipe away the tears you cry

14. Who Will You Be?

You share our heartbeat
But what else will we share to?
Will you laugh like me?
Will your eyes be green or brown or blue?
Will you smile at strangers
Or will you be shy?
Will you let your heart glide
Or be afraid to fly?
Will you love to read
Or will you prefer to run?
Will you jump in winter snow
Or thrive in the sun?
These months go by fast
But equally slow
As I ponder all the questions
Whose answers I will soon know
There's one thing I am sure
You are my heart beat
The notes etched in my soul
The melody in my head on repeat

15. First Tears

Your first cry
Unraveled all I knew
I was remade
I exist to love you
Days are often a blur
Tears, laugher, need
But when I look at you
My heart is pleased
Like how God looks at his creation
And he could not love it more
I do not know
How I ever thought of love before
When God made this world
He looked and he stood
He smiled and he loved
For what he had made was good
This is how God felt
When he made you through me
He looked at you like I do
Unconditional love is all we see

16. First Smiles

I've never felt love like I do right now
You are our greatest wish fulfilled
We are whole because of your heartbeat
Your perfect smile, just as God willed
The way your eyes alight
When they lock with mine
Leave me with nothing but inspiration
Every day a new line
About how perfect you are
My heart cannot love more than this
Then you smile and I am wrong
Your smile is complete bliss

17. Zaniya

We named you forever and always
That's how long we'll love you
That's how long God will hold you
In his heart too
We named you after God's Grace
Because that's his greatest gift
We named you after God's most beautiful path
So you're watched over with every foot you lift
With every step you take
Never forget what God has done
For he made you, painted your heart
With the same strokes as the sun
So shine bright my beautiful girl
Be unapologetically you
Praise God for what he has done
And what He is yet to do

18. Scars Etched Upon My Skin

These scars etched upon my skin
Represent the journey we share
For you, I'd lay down my life
I'd do anything to show you I care
My scars are the proof
Of the heartbeat interwoven with mine
That lived within me
Getting stronger with time
These scars engraved on my skin
May fade but will never be gone
They're a testament
To my perfect miracle born
These scars are the life I prayed for
The love I ached to know
The sacrifice I'd make over and over
To see the bloom of the seeds we sow

19. Zaniya's Prayer

My beautiful daughter
This is your prayer
I pray you always seek justice
And have a soul full of care
I pray you always follow your heart
But let your head have a say
I pray that you know you're loved
Every second of every day
May you be levelheaded
Yet fiercely strong willed
I pray you're heart is thankful
And Holy Spirit filled
Most of all I pray you know
Exactly who you are
And how you came from the One
Who painted the brightest star
You were hand crafted, intricately painted
Every day I will pray this again
You are God's masterpiece
And all the angels sang, Amen

20. Whisper's in the Night

I whisper to the night
As she sleeps in my arms
My finger caught
In her tiny clenched palms
Lord, if tears ever fall
Or the clouds shadow her sun
Give her strength to see
that only battles fought, can be won
Give her the wisdom to know
When she should stand and fight
And when to walk away
Give her peace in what is right
Lord, make her strong
Give her love without fear
Walk with her no matter the direction
Keep her heart near
Lord, when I am no longer close
A memory of maternity
Let her never forget
That I will love her through eternity
Until that I time
I will forever pray
Watch over my daughter
May she find joy in every day

21. Right By Your Side

The last thing I have to say is
You're my everything, my forever
The family we've created
My greatest endeavour
I couldn't love you more
Not even if I tried
Just look and you will find me
Right by your side